— COMPLIANCE —

CHRONICLES

STORIES EVERY ENTREPRENEUR MUST HEAR

By

CA MANISH BANSAL

ABOUT THE AUTHOR

CA Manish Bansal is a qualified Chartered Accountant with extensive expertise in **GST litigation, advisory, and internal auditing**.

With over 12 years of hands-on experience, he has successfully represented clients before various tax authorities and appellate forums, helping businesses navigate the complexities of indirect tax laws with clarity and confidence.

Known for his sharp analytical skills and practical approach, he has also played a pivotal role in strengthening internal control systems and compliance frameworks across diverse industries.

His commitment to ethical practice, deep understanding of regulatory landscapes, and passion for knowledge-sharing have made him a trusted advisor to both emerging enterprises and established corporations.

Through *Compliance Chronicles*, he brings together real-world insights and compelling narratives from the frontline of

Compliance, offering valuable lessons every entrepreneur and professional should know.

WHY THIS BOOK?

Compliance Chronicles: Stories Every Entrepreneur Should Hear is not just a book—it's a journey into the often-overlooked world of business compliance, brought to life through compelling real-life narratives and professional insights.

As rules and regulations become stricter and there's less room for mistakes, this book is a great reminder that following the rules isn't just about avoiding fines. It's really about building trust, being sustainable, and setting up for long-term success.

Written by a senior Chartered Accountant with years of hands-on experience in **GST litigation, compliance strategy, and internal audits**, this book explains the importance of timely Compliance and the impacts of non-compliance through thought-provoking stories. Each chapter contains unique experiences, real-life situations, illustrations, and examples of how entrepreneurs and business owners have either fallen short or risen strongly based on their approach to Compliance.

The book goes beyond checklists and creates awareness to explore:

- The hidden risks of ignorance and shortcuts

- The real cost of non-compliance—beyond just monetary penalties

- How a compliance-first culture can become a competitive edge

- The mindset shift required to treat regulations as opportunities, not obstacles

- Strategies to align Compliance with business objectives without sacrificing agility

Whether you're running a startup, managing a growing enterprise, or advising clients as a finance professional, *Compliance Chronicles* equips you with practical wisdom, relatable experiences, and the motivation to do business the right way.

It is a must-read for anyone who wants to understand not just **what** Compliance is but **why** it matters—and how it can shape the future of modern businesses.

ACKNOWLEDGEMENTS

I firmly believe that the best planning is done by the almighty, and no matter what you are going through, his planning always supersedes your planning for you. Holding my hand and blessing me always, GOD has always been kind to me. Shaping my personal and professional life so beautifully and now providing me an opportunity to be an Author... one can't ask for more. I am grateful to GOD and dedicate this book to the Almighty. "हे ईश्वर, आपका धन्यवाद "

Nothing would have been possible without the blessings of my parents, my father, Mr. Pramod Kumar Bansal, and my mother, Mrs. Aruna Bansal. Everything I am and everything I do is because of them. They've supported every decision I've made, always selflessly. Thank you for always being there.

This book would not have been possible without the unwavering pillar of strength, my wife, Mrs. Anjali Bansal. Your understanding through tight deadlines, your encouragement through long hours, and your belief in me compelled me to believe that I can actually be an author.

Thank you for always supporting me in every thick and thin of life. To my daughter, Ms. Himanshi Bansal, you are a constant source of joy and inspiration. Your endless curiosity and all your questions about the book kept pushing me to finish it. I hope one day you'll read it and feel proud.

Writing a book was never in my wildest dreams, but thanks to my mentor and coach, Mr. Gaurav Arora, Sir. He is the person who seeded the idea in my mind to write the book. He believed in me before I believed in myself.

Not only this, but he also gave his constant guidance, framework, and, most preciously, his time in this journey of book writing. He understood our problem of being occupied in the office, and then he introduced a special window of 3 hours (5 AM to 8 AM) in the morning just for writing the book.

The magical part was that he was present all the time during the book writing. I present my whole-hearted gratitude to Gaurav Arora, Sir, without whom this book would not have been possible.

I want to thank my **clients and colleagues**, whose real-world challenges and experiences have inspired many of the stories shared in this book. Their trust, conversations, and case histories have shaped not only this narrative but also my understanding of the evolving landscape of Compliance.

I want to express my gratitude to my **mentors and senior colleagues in the profession**, who guided me early in my career and helped me develop a strong foundation in GST litigation. Your wisdom continues to resonate through every consultation I undertake.

I want to express my sincere appreciation to my team, especially my partner, CA Dhruv Goyal, whose support in research, documentation, and logistics helped keep this project moving.

I want to express my sincere gratitude to my **reviewers, Puneet Agarwal, Ankit Garg, Akshay Jain, and Anirudh Lal**, whose valuable feedback, thoughtful suggestions, and a keen eye for detail greatly enhanced the quality of this book. Your time, expertise, and constructive critique helped refine the content and ensure it delivers clarity, relevance, and impact to its readers.

Finally, to the **readers** — entrepreneurs, professionals, and students thank you for choosing this book. May these Chronicles offer you clarity, caution, and confidence as you navigate the path of doing business the right way.

With sincere gratitude,

CA Manish Bansal

DISCLAIMER

This book contains narratives, case studies, and chronicles that are inspired by real-life situations and experiences. While some of the events, circumstances, and business challenges presented may reflect actual occurrences, they have been adapted or fictionalized for the purpose of illustration, education, or storytelling. Any resemblance to specific individuals, clients, businesses, officers, or institutions—past or present—is purely coincidental unless explicitly stated.

To maintain ethical standards and uphold confidentiality, the names, locations, roles, and identifying details of all individuals and organizations have been altered or omitted. The intention is not to disclose any proprietary or personal information but to share insights, lessons, and transformative ideas in a way that respects privacy and professional boundaries.

The characters and dialogues presented are crafted to convey key messages and may include composite profiles based on multiple real-life experiences. Readers are encouraged to focus on the broader takeaways rather than on specific interpretations or assumptions about the people or companies referenced.

This book does not intend to harm, defame, or misrepresent any individual or organization. All efforts have been made to ensure integrity and discretion throughout.

TABLE OF CONTENTS

CHAPTER 1

3Ws OF COMPLIANCE

"After years apart, Prithvi and Akash—two friends turned entrepreneurs—were finally meeting again. Though bound by friendship, their journey in business had gone down divergent roads, shaped by distinctly different mindsets and approaches to success."

Prithvi just got a call from the GST Department, and he learned that a new notice had been issued against his firm. Prithvi dejectedly disconnected the call and decided to meet his childhood friend Akash, who was also an entrepreneur and had connections in the GST office. Prithvi was disturbed since he was receiving notices frequently from the GST Department.

Upon reaching Akash's office, Prithvi found that his friend was eagerly waiting for him. They reunited with great enthusiasm, celebrating the moment with warmth and shared joy, diving into memories and even sharing their life journeys. Akash observed that Prithvi acted normally all the time, but there was a miss. Something was surely off.

"What's the matter, Prithvi? " Akash suddenly asked. Prithvi, smiling, replied, 'So, you got me as always.'

A: Tell me, what's wrong?

The moment Akash asked this, Prithvi poured his heart out and said:

P: For the past few months, I have been getting regular notices from the GST Department, and I find it difficult to handle them anymore. This government is not at all business-friendly, and they want to increase their revenue collection. A small businessman like me can't survive in these conditions anymore. The impact of ongoing litigations is such that my business operations are also being affected. *"I know you're friends with some GST officers," he said, his voice low and urgent. "I need your help — get me out of this mess. That's all I have thought about lately. My mind... won't stop."*

A: Relax, Prithvi. First of all, this is not the fault of the government. Rules and Regulations are the same all over India for every businessman. No matter whether you are a small businessman or a business giant, the rules and their implications are the same for all. Moreover, please get in touch with my chartered accountant (CA), Mr. Vikas, since he is the perfect person to guide you in this matter.

P: But why do we need a CA when you have a direct connection in the department?

A: I agree that I know some officers personally, but only the CA can tell us why you are getting notices so frequently and what the best approach to handle them should be. So, let me call my CA and tell him everything in detail.

Prithvi sounded convinced. He had a telephone conversation with Vikas and shared all the notices and details he had asked for. Prithvi became relaxed listening to our conversation and even made an appointment with Vikas for the very next day. He was relaxed now, and he thanked his friend Akash for getting him connected to Vikas.

The next day, Prithvi reached the CA's office and discussed the notices he had received. Vikas asked Prithvi who filed the GST Returns? Prithvi replied that since it was the starting phase of the business, the firm's accountant himself filed the GST Returns. Vikas then told him that there were discrepancies in the returns filed by the accountant and that he was also a regular non-compliant dealer.

Pritithvi was shocked to learn this and requested Vikas to tell him more details. Vikas replied that there was a delay in filing the returns, and sometimes, the data declared in the returns was mismatched with the information available at the portal. You are a regular non-compliant. Prithvi looked confused, so Vikas decided to make Prithvi aware of the 3 W's of Compliance. Vikas said, If you want success and growth in your business, always remember the 3 W's of Compliance.

First, **W**hat is Compliance?

Second, **W**hy is Compliance necessary?

The third is **W**hen Compliance needs to be done.

Firstly, Compliance means following the rules and regulations set by the authorities you are registered with. If you are registered with GST, you are required to follow the rules and regulations set by the GST authorities.

Secondly, Compliance is required since all Compliance is purpose-driven. The government/authorities prepare and set the framework for the smooth exchange and flow of data/transactions among business owners and other related organizations in the economy. So, if we don't comply with the rules and regulations, the smooth flow of data/transactions gets adversely affected. For example, If dealer "A," who is registered under GST, issues a tax invoice to other businessmen "B" and "A" fails to file the GSTR-1 as prescribed by the GST Authorities, the purchaser "B" will not be able to get the benefit of GST paid to "A." Therefore, Compliance is essential for achieving the purpose of the framework prepared by the authorities.

Thirdly, compliance must be achieved within the time limits prescribed by the authorities. In fact, every entrepreneur must try to complete the Compliance before the last date. If you fail to comply even for a single day, you will be counted as non-compliant only.

"So, Prithvi," Akash said with a knowing smile, "I think you finally understand the importance of compliance."

And he did.

For the first time in days, everything seemed clear. But instead of feeling content, a new feeling began to stir in him — curiosity. He wanted to dig deeper, to truly understand the world of Compliance and what happened when one strayed from it.

What if someone is non-compliant due to a genuine reason? Is the government biased in making the laws and rules related to Compliance? Can a non-compliant convert into a compliant one? And if yes, how? How can a dealer become Non-Compliant? Can a businessman create such a system that there is never a non-compliance? There was a flurry of such questions in his mind. Therefore, he requested Mr. Vikas to enlighten him in depth about non-compliance. Vikas gracefully accepted the request and asked Prithvi to visit him on Saturday for a detailed session to understand everything related to Non-compliance.

CHAPTER 2

COMMON REASONS FOR NON-COMPLIANCE

It's 11:00 AM!!! Curious Prithvi was sitting with Mr. Vikas to learn more about Non-Compliance.

P: Sir, the knowledge you shared in the previous meeting sparked my curiosity about what mistakes entrepreneurs like me usually make in the absence of proper guidance.

V: Prithviji, first of all, I appreciate the fact that you are eager to learn new things or new aspects about Non-Compliance to scale your business. Now, let me discuss a few possible reasons for non-compliance that I came across during my practice:

a) <u>**Lack of Education/ Ignorance of Law:**</u> One of the primary reasons for non-compliance is the absence of proper awareness or understanding of applicable laws and regulations. There are significant numbers of business owners who are not educated, and no efforts are made by either the revenue authorities or professional bodies to educate such business owners regarding the timelines and basic compliances to be done. It has been observed that most of these business owners apply for GST Registrations to make them eligible to enter into tenders, and their concern is limited to that only. Post-registration compliances are done only to maintain the registration active, and in such cases, one can't expect that compliances are done actively/regularly.

In addition to the above, it has been widely observed that most of the unaware business owners apply for GST Registrations to complete the mandatory requirement of documents for opening a current account. As per the guidelines, maximum proprietorship concerns require a minimum of one registration with a Business Entity Name, and maximum business owners go for GST Registrations, and they are not aware of the monthly GST Return filings and other precautions to be taken care of. The focus was to open the current account. When the business owners actually try to start the business, they find themselves in a dilemma, i.e., whether to use the funds to execute the newly received work orders or to use the funds to pay the GST liability on account of non-compliance. In this way, the first step towards the commencement of business goes awry, and it derails the business's scaling from the initial point.

Therefore, we recommend that every business owner be aware of all the compliances related to any registration they are going to enter.

b) **<u>Careless Mindset:</u>** Another major concern is the mindset of business leaders, who wait for the last date for tax payment, even if they are capable of paying the tax earlier than the last date. They fail to consider the unforeseen uncertainties that may delay the payment of taxes from the timeline provided by the law. Let me share a real-life experience:

*"One of my clients paid the taxes (GST) on the 20th of the month, and the amount got debited from the bank account, but at the GST Portal, the status of the payment was **"Awaiting payment confirmation from the bank"** for the whole day and the payment was approved on 21st and hence the client who has paid the*

I always advise my clients to pay the due taxes a day before the due date to avoid any interest, late fees, and avoidable litigation. **<u>"Timely tax payments aren't a burden — they're a mark of a smart business."</u>**

I have noticed one more kind of default, and the reason for the same is being careless only, and that default ignores the communications received from the revenue authorities. Ignoring communications can lead not only to non-compliance but also to missed opportunities for timely rectification at the departmental level. As a result, business owners may be compelled to approach the High Courts to seek relief, which could have been avoided with prompt action. Let me share two real-life instances where ignoring the communications from the department led to the high court seeking relief from an ex parte order passed by the department.

"In the first instance, one of our clients failed to share the mail containing the dates for the hearing of the assessment proceedings, including multiple reminders for the same. Not only this, but he also failed to share the mail containing the ex-parte order (an order which has been passed by the revenue authorities where the assessee

failed to attend the proceedings) and due to the same time for filing the appeal against the same has been lapsed and there is no option left other than moving to the high court for filing the appeal against the order passed and seeking the relief."

"In the second instance, the client filed for cancellation of registration, and the GST Department approved it. After getting the cancellation application approved, the business owners have received multiple notices along with reminders to attend the assessment proceedings. Still, they completely ignored all the communications, resulting in receiving the order for heavy demands. When we addressed the matter, we found that it was a simple notice, and if we had received it on time, the assessment proceedings could easily have been dropped without depositing a single penny."

Numerous instances similar to the above exist, and in all of them, the business owners have to pay a heavy amount of taxes, interest, and penalties. Such instances result not only in monetary losses but also in intense mental agony. So, we suggest that business leaders remain alert about all the communications received from the revenue authorities.

c) <u>**Lack of Integrity:**</u> I always suggest to clients that if they fail to respect the timelines provided by law or any other non-compliance has been done, then always attach a penalty for yourself so that you don't repeat the same mistake. However, I found that the majority of them consider it a one-time default/ first default and justify their approach by saying that we have paid the interest and late fee to the government, so why add more burden for the same mistake? I partially agree that you paid the interest and penalty to the government, but if you don't want to repeat these mistakes, attach a financial burden for you or the person responsible for the non-compliance so that the repetition of such acts can be avoided. A few of my clients have applied the same, and they have been fully compliant for many years.

d) **<u>Financial Crunch:</u>** In the majority of the instances I came across, the excuse was that we are a compliant company/ firm, but due to a shortage of funds, we are not able to pay the taxes on time. This is an absolute blunder since the government charges interest on late payment of taxes at 18% p.a. while the banks provide the funds to the business owners at 12-14%. So, whenever you are short of funds, please take a loan at the prevailing lending rate and pay the taxes on time so that you avoid being non-compliant.

Also, we share one more approach related to the planning of tax payments with our clients, and our clients appreciate that approach. "We know that the payment you received includes the amount of goods/services provided and the amount of GST charged. So, keep the amount of GST charged in your bank account and use the same to discharge the tax liability, especially for the service providers." However, if you have calculated the tentative amount of output tax liability, then reserve that amount and use the surplus amount available in your bank account.

Moreover, I always advise my business owners to calculate the GST output liability at the end of every month so that they have a fair idea of their probable tax liability for that month. I also suggest they keep a check on the flow of funds/cash flow on a regular basis so that a situation like a financial crunch can be avoided.

e) **<u>Ignorance about Consequences:</u>** Generally, business owners have the mindset that non-compliance can be made good by paying penal interest and late fees. However, what they don't know is that non-compliance might attract notices from the GST Department. Revenue authorities in the GST Department keep records of every error made by business owners, and they keep a close eye on regular defaulters. Entrepreneurs are ignorant of the fact that revenue authorities are using various tools generated and operated by Artificial Intelligence (AI), which not only follow the patterns of business transactions but also keep an eye on the list of vendors with

which they are dealing. So, I always recommend that my clients be compliant, and being compliant will always be a shield against unwanted notices from the GST department. It should be noted that non-compliance has monetary and non-monetary impacts on the business.

    f) **<u>Emergency Situation:</u>** Sometimes, the clients fail to pay the taxes on time, or any other type of non-compliance may occur due to severe health conditions or any other extreme adverse situations. In such cases, we suggest that our clients keep the documentation for every default made, mentioning each detail and the causes of the non-compliance. So that, in case of receipt of the notice, we can produce the trail of the events causing the non-compliance and our actions to make the default good. In the eyes of the law, intention plays an important role in the assessment proceedings. If we establish that the non-compliance is unintentional, then the assessing authorities may grant relief, and vice versa. Therefore, keeping the documentation for every irregular event as per the provisions of the law is highly recommended.

Hopefully, I succeed in explaining the possible common reasons for non-compliance, "Vikas said.

Surely, replied Prithvi.

P: But I would like to know what the worst-case scenario may be in case of non-compliance, as you mentioned that it has both monetary and non-monetary impacts.

Why not??? Let's have some coffee and continue the discussion there. Replied Vikas.

CHAPTER 3

HOW GRAVE NON-COMPLIANCE CAN BE

As the session continued, Prithvi showed interest in learning about the impacts of non-compliance and what can happen at the extreme level.

V: Before I discuss the monetary impacts of non-compliance, let me first discuss the non-monetary impacts.

Non-Monetary Impacts of Non-Compliance

1. *Business Reputation is at stake.*

When a business idea first takes shape in the mind of the business owner, the very first goal is to make it a famous name in the market. *"A name that will command respect as well as goodwill and that too of such a high level that every person would like to work with us."* This is the statement that must have crossed the mind of every business owner at some point in their business, i.e., maybe at commencement, at the time of expansion, or after achieving a few significant landmarks, maybe in terms of money, having Fortune 50 companies as your client, etc. The point is that making your business a respectable name is a dream of every business owner. This very dream of every business owner can quickly fall apart due to non-compliance, no matter the reason. Every non-compliance raises questions over the intention of the business concern, and you easily fall under the suspected or defaulter list of the government, vendors, banks, etc.

We always guide our clients so that every prospective client can check the GST compliance chart* and that if you are non-compliant, you are easily placed below the compliant business owners in the list of probable vendors. Your reputation in the market takes a hit when people focus more on your non-compliance than on your accomplishments. *In any meeting, achievements are discussed only after the discussion of non-compliance comes to an end.*

Now, consider a scenario where you established a company 5 years ago, and after 5 years of business, you now require credit facilities from the bank to scale your existing business. Still, at the time of due diligence, you came to know that the bank has declined your application for exposure due to any of the following reasons:

a) Being a regular late Income Tax Return filer,

b) Being a regular GST Return Defaulter,

c) Multiple notices have been issued to you for non-compliance

Compliance Chart is available on page number 33

We know that every business owner will try to convince the bank that the above defaults were due to any of the possible business reasons, but **not every business owner can compel the bank to buy their argument.** Each default or non-compliance puts a question mark on the intention of the business owner. No matter how genuine your causes of non-compliance were, you have to rely on the lender's wishes. Moreover, suppose the bank agreed to provide you with the exposure. In that case, they will always charge a higher rate of interest since the risk rating has already considered the risk of non-payment or late payment of the exposed amount, which arises due to non-compliance.

The above scenario, which I shared with you, was actually faced by one of our clients. Our client used to pay the taxes generally after the due date.

Every instance of non-compliance can damage your brand's reputation so severely that rebuilding it may require twice the effort.

2. <u>Loss of Productivity</u>

The most underrated impact of non-compliance is the Loss of productivity in business operations due to the **unrest and botheration** it causes in the mind. It's a natural phenomenon that if there is a botheration in your mind, no matter how hard you try to ignore it, you will always find it knocking on the peaceful space in the mind, creating some unease. The moment your mind seems to be relaxed, and you are not focused to the complete degree, the botheration seeps into the mind. It affects the creativity, productivity, and beauty of the thought process, which ultimately impacts decision-making and finally becomes a constraint to quality actions.

This improper decision-making adversely impacts operations

and results. The worst part is that this may continue for a long duration. The reason is that the skill to handle such botheration without letting it affect one's thought process is difficult to develop.

The business owners never assess the cost of delay in decision-making or delay in operations. For example, in the case of manufacturing units, if the quality of goods manufactured is affected and the vendors reject the same or you fail to meet the expectations of the purchaser, then either the goods will be rejected, or the manufacturer will have to re-manufacture the goods. In both scenarios, the cost will increase, and eventually, the margin of the business will be lower. Such costings are not considered or calculated, and in most cases, such losses are ignored.

The adverse impact on productivity, quality, decision-making, and delays in operations increases the cost of the business. These costs are invisible losses to the business and result.

Non-compliance can have a deadly impact on the business. So, one must consider the above factors and refrain from engaging in non-compliance.

3. _Invitation to Litigation_

Mr. Prithvi, we encountered numerous business owners who complained that they were receiving regular notices from the GST Department despite paying the due taxes correctly and regularly. You also said the same thing when you contacted me for the first time. But answer me a question: How many times did your CA inform you that the notice you received was totally wrong and no amount of tax, interest, or penalty was payable against it?

Almost none, Vikas Sir. I mean, we have paid the tax and interest, sometimes a penalty also, against the notices we received. Replied Prithvi.

V: It means none of the notices you received were wrongly generated. Every notice was issued as there was some sort of non-compliance on your part, maybe non-filing of prescribed returns, excess Input Tax Credit has been availed, a short declaration of output liability, or maybe missing the deadline for filing the returns.

P: Yes, Sir, we made mistakes, but that happened because we were not completely aware that all those things needed to be taken care of.

V: First of all, Prithvi, as a business owner, you are not allowed to take shelter under the umbrella of being unaware of the law. Whenever you enter into transactions that are new to you or involve technical decision-making, you must seek consultancy from professionals and become aware. Being unaware of the law keeps you short of being an impactful business owner.

Now, get back to the part of your statement in which you accepted that there were mistakes on your part and notices were issued to address those mistakes. No matter whether those gaps were intentional or not, you become a defaulter in the eyes of the law and, therefore, liable to be questioned by the department. Gaps created either by not providing complete information in return, not filing the return on time, or by any other non-compliance compel the revenue authorities to keep an eye on your business conduct, and you attract unwanted litigation.

Any notice received from the GST department involves two aspects of monetary losses. The first aspect of money outflow is the amount of interest and penalty to be paid. The due taxes and the second aspect of money outflow are professional charges to be paid to the person who will appear before the court on your behalf.

So, suppose you pay taxes correctly and enter into business transactions cautiously. In that case, there are higher chances that you will not receive the notice, and if you still receive the notice, your professional will be at ease in getting the assessment done in your favor. So, I request that business owners do business vigilantly and always keep in mind that every mistake counts, and every mistake might attract significant monetary losses in the form of interest, penalty, and professional charges.

4. *Unavoidable Mental Agony*

Non-compliance is directly proportional to mental agony. The intensity of mental agony depends on the time gap between the event of non-compliance and the event of making the non-compliance good. In simple words, if non-compliance is made good immediately after the occurrence of non-compliance, the defaulter can limit the monetary loss as well as the mental agony.

The first reaction of the majority of the business owners after receiving the notice is ***Why did I receive this notice ?" "How will this issue be resolved?" and "How much money will I end*** *up losing?"* Business owners get the answers to the first two questions very easily and somehow get at ease with these queries in their minds. Still, the last question bothers them the most since the proceedings take time to conclude, and one is not able to assess how much they have to pay before getting the order passed. So, the third question bothers business owners the most, and when the amount involved in the notice is huge, then this also becomes the reason for loss of peace of mind and, sometimes, loss of sleep. If any question remains unanswered for a long time, it can create a sense of uncertainty and incompleteness, leading to frustration and hindering intellectual progress. Also, this feeling of uncertainty can prevent a person from understanding the problem-solving concept, resulting in stagnation in learning or problem-solving and potentially missed opportunities for business growth.

Moreover, Unanswered questions can lead to feelings of inadequacy, confusion, and even anxiety, especially if the questions are related to important or pressing issues. The continuous search for answers to the uncertainty and anxiety might affect their health, too. Let me share a real-life incident with you.

One of my clients received a notice for not filing an income tax return for the year 2019-20. He shared the notice with me and started asking questions related to the Notice right away. Same questions as mentioned above. For the first two questions, I replied to him after going through the notice, and the immediate response from the client was, "Ok, Sir, you are the best person to handle the notice, so please play your part, but give me an idea of judgment. Whether we will get the full relief, partial relief, or no relief will be provided?" I assured him that we would take care of the same, and since the proceedings are faceless and it will take time to conclude the assessment proceedings, I will not be able to address the last question at an early stage. The proceedings came to an end after 8 months, and every time we communicated, I sensed that the client wanted to get that last question answered. Although we got the order passed in favor of the client, that means an order was passed where no amount was to be deposited by our client; still, our client has to go through uncertainty and anxiety for such a long period of 8 months. I remember him acknowledging in one of our communications that "Every time I am not working, my mind goes to the notice, and a question pops up – Don't know, what will happen?"

Let me add a version to the story that, in case a demand order had been passed demanding a significant amount and levying interest and penalty, the period of mental unrest would have been extended. So, the impact of such increased mental stress or anxiety due to the notices can't be monetized, but it is a proven fact that increased mental stress significantly affects a person's health.

5. *Closure of Business*

When I say non-compliance may lead to business closure, you might feel that I am speaking out loud to create a context. But this is true, and one of my clients had to shut down one of his manufacturing units due to non-compliance. Let me share the whole incident with you so that you can see how grave non-compliance can be.

One of my clients who deals in the manufacturing of perishable items has a manufacturing unit located in Greater Noida. In December 2019, a vehicle carrying his raw material was stopped by the GST Mobile Squad for checking. While all the documents with the goods in the vehicle were up to the mark, the department decided to detain the vehicle as our client had non-compliance. During the proceedings of releasing the vehicle, the GST department asked the client to share some information about the last few purchases and sales. While analyzing the data, the department formed an opinion that the assessee doesn't keep the stock records properly and that there must be some serious non-compliance. The department decided to search the client's business premises, and the search was subsequently carried out. A few gaps were found, and the department seized the manufacturing plant. Since the product was a perishable and temperature-controlled item, the client paid the demand assessed so that the manufacturing plant could be functional as soon as possible. The plant became functional, but COVID-19 arrived in March 2020. After the government lifted the restrictions with respect to COVID precautions, the offices resumed. The plant became operational after a gap of a few months. Still, my client received a flurry of notices with respect to the assessment proceedings of the search conducted, as well as many other notices for different tax periods for assessment purposes. The client was sailing in two boats; one was to resume the business and scale the production to meet the expenses after Covid, and on the other hand, he was stuck with a number of notices received by him. We were pursuing litigation proceedings, but the department started a new practice, i.e., frequent visits to the plant on the basis of the history of non-compliance. After grinding for a good one and a half years, the assessee shut down the manufacturing plant and sold the factory; this was the whole scenario.

Now, let me share my background working in the GST department for such an aggressive approach against my client. We came to know that the assessee used to cancel E-way Bills frequently. Also, the volume of the transaction was heavy, but the tax deposited against the same was minimal. A few more irregularities were found, and the department marked my client as a Red Flag dealer as he was a repeat defaulter in the eyes of the law. The department was keeping an eye on every detail he submitted and every activity he performed on the GST Portal. The department studied the pattern of business conduct and suspected that information filed through returns was incomplete and incorrect. This triggered a whole course of action taken by the GST department to evaluate, investigate, and make suitable recoveries.

If I summarize the whole sequence of events, we can say that the dealer was compliant as per his understanding, while a red flag dealer means a risky dealer in the eyes of the law due to non-compliance. When the GST department started the assessment and recovery proceedings, the dealer found himself unable to concentrate on the business due to the never-ending litigations and decided to close the business to avoid further litigation. You can easily connect the dots of how non-compliance dented the reputation of the business, loss of productivity in the business, unwanted, never-ending litigations were initiated, and a high level of mental stress was there that closing a business plant seemed to be easier than continuing with the litigations.

"Therefore, it is crucial to take compliance seriously and avoid situations that could impact your business so severely that its continuity is put at risk."

V: From the above discussion, I conveyed the impacts of non-compliance, which result in losses other than monetary loss. I am sure you must have gotten a fair idea of monetary losses from the above, but still, let me explain the monetary impacts of non-compliance.

Monetary Impacts of Non-Compliance

When it comes to the monetary impacts of non-compliance, be

sure that it reduces the business's profit margins.

Whatever extra cost is there, whether in the form of interest and penalty, professional charges, or the opportunity cost of the money paid by you to get rid of the notice received by you, it certainly reduces the profit margin of the business.

You must be aware of the two aspects of money outflow, "interest and penalty" and "professional charges," but have you ever calculated the opportunity cost of the money you paid in lieu of non-compliance?

The opportunity cost of money is the potential benefit or return foregone when money is used to pay interest, penalties, and professional charges instead of for business purposes.

For example, suppose the business owner has to pay the interest and penalty of Rs. 5 lakhs while complying with the notice.

In that case, the owner analyzes the fact that if these 5 lakh rupees had been used in the business, what return would he have earned from it?

That loss of return on these five lakh rupees is the opportunity cost of the same.

"Making an Alliance with Compliance is the only way to immunize your business from the impacts of non-compliance."

P: Vikas, you made me dive so deep into the impact of non-compliance that it will take time to sink in with my thought process. In addition to that, I am unable to analyze how many non-compliances I might have committed to date and how I am going to deal with their consequences.

V: Prithvi, I intended to make you aware of how dangerous non-compliance can be. If you are bothered by it, it means your mind is active and ready to learn about the steps to be taken to avoid it. So, we are going to discuss a few myths about non-compliance that commonly prevail in the business owner's thought process.

Now, Prithvi noticed that his mind was in ultra-active mode, and he was eager to learn about the myths and precautions to be taken to avoid non-compliance.

Basically, he found himself in a very receptive mode, eager like a child to learn new aspects of business routine that would allow him to scale without the intervention of the GST department.

CHAPTER 4

BREAKING THE LIES

V: Do you know Prithvi? There is a trait in human nature that whenever you commit a mistake, you always need someone to blame. We don't easily accept that it is my fault, I am fully responsible for this, and I will take care of it. What we do, in actuality, is whenever the situation goes awry, we try to pull ourselves neat and clean and try to blame others for that situation. Let me share an incident:

The Blame Game: A Real Incident

One day, I got a call from one of my clients who was furious and questioned the efficiency of my team since one of his buyers was complaining that he was unable to claim the Input tax credit for the bill that my client issued to that buyer. I got that call in March 2025, and the bill in question belongs to February 2024. I asked my client that you must have received a detailed GSTR-1 for the period 2023-24 from my office for scrutiny purposes. Have you checked the same? Was this invoice available on that sheet, or was it missing? My client hesitantly said he did not get the time to check the sheet in spite of multiple reminders from my office. I said since the timeline of amending or adding any invoice pertaining to 2023-24 has lapsed, no amendments can be done, and the purpose of sharing the detailed GST report for scrutiny was the same, that in case any invoice requires amendment, it can be done before the timeline lapses. But you failed to fulfill your duty, and now you are blaming my team for the mistake, so let me be very clear that we share the sheet with the client and send three reminders to check the sheet and inform us well before the timeline so that if any changes can be incorporated in the GST Returns. The client acknowledged his mistake and assured me he would be more proactive going forward to avoid similar situations.

This incident highlights a common psychological pattern—when confronted with a mistake, our first instinct is often to deflect responsibility instead of owning the mistake.

Let me discuss a few common myths that business owners use

to comfort themselves when they find themselves being non-compliant:

1. <u>Wrong government policies</u>

This is the most common outcry from business owners that government policies are not in alignment with the business, and due to this, we find it difficult to comply with them. For example, the business owner contested that the credit period is for 60 days, and we receive our payment within 50 days of issuance of the invoice. Still, we have to pay the taxes by the 20th of the succeeding month, so the government should collect the tax after receipt of the payment. This contention of the business owner actually covers a pain point of working.

Capital crunch, but vis-à-vis, it is impractical to link the GST collection with the receipt of the payments. The government drafts and implements the policy after thorough research and considers all the factors together. Government policies are purpose-driven, and they are the same for all. Since the policies are the same for all and every business owner is bound by these, considering that the government policies are at fault and blaming the same for non-compliance is not a sign of a good business mindset. Accept the policies, draft the business procedures considering the government policies, and be a compliant business owner; that should be the focus instead of blaming the government for its policies. Like in the above example, if the business owner manages its cash flows and fixes the payment schedule in such a way that working capital can be avoided and the business is cash-rich during the due date for payment of taxes, then there will be no impact of gaps in the timeline for receiving the payment from the buyer and due date for payment of taxes. So, plan the business procedures in accordance with the due date of compliance for the smooth functioning of the business entities.

2. <u>Non-availability of funds to pay taxes</u>

If the business owner is short of funds and decides to delay the payment of taxes, please be aware that the government charges 18% p.a. interest from the first day of default. In comparison, the business loan available from the bank is supposedly at 12%. So if you borrow the money from the bank and pay the taxes, you save approximately. 6%, and by doing the same, you not only put yourself off the list of defaulters but also mitigate the risk of receiving a notice from the department. Again, payment of taxes on time is as important as getting a client for business. So, if you prioritize the payment of taxes with that much importance, you will be able to pay the taxes on time; it's all about the mindset. Dragging the payment of taxes up to the last possible date is just multiplying the interest and penal cost over the same period. So, be smart and choose to pay the taxes on time instead of procrastinating.

3. It's easy to get away with non-compliance

We have come across a lot of business owners who proudly declare that we have committed mistakes in our businesses, and to date, not a single notice has been received, so it's very easy to get away with non-compliance. I reply to them to always keep praying that you don't receive any notice since if you receive the notice from the department and you know you have committed mistakes, you will not be able to defend yourself. You will be paying a hefty amount of interest and penalty. Most of them replied that the last day for issuance of notice had lapsed, and they were safe now. To which my response was, Sir, the last day has lapsed for the assessment proceedings only where the department believes that the fault was unintentional. If the department believes that you are a willful defaulter, they will reach out to you and investigate you, and in case of fraud or misrepresentation, there is no escape route in the GST Act 2017. Therefore, it is never easy to get away with non-compliance, especially when you have committed the same offense intentionally.

4. <u>The government doesn't have time to track small firms.</u>

A number of business owners tend to form multiple firms and divide the business into multiple firms so that the quantum of business is divided into small firms. No single firm is highlighted as a giant firm in the eyes of the department. In this case, I always suggest to my client that no matter what the size of your firm is, if you are a compliant business entity, you need not worry about the GST department and focus on scaling the business rather than chasing the course of action of the department. The main reason for my suggestion is that there is no manual system for tracking the turnover and conduct of the business. The government has developed Artificial Intelligence systems where this software tracks business patterns and rates the business on the basis of risk factors, considering the filing patterns, fluctuation in sales, quality of ITC claims, etc. Any activity of yours that is unusual to the pattern of the business sends an alarm to the government, and you automatically fall into the category of a risky business dealer. So, the AI is rating the business on the basis of the patterns, not the turnover; therefore, you can't guarantee that if the business is small, the government can't track you. If any discrepancies are detected, the system automatically flags the data for government action. In this environment, the size of your firm is irrelevant—what truly matters is how you conduct your business.

5. <u>**Only paying the interest and penalty doesn't make you a compliant dealer.**</u>

It's a common tendency to believe that once you have paid the interest and penalty related to the default, the non-compliant dealer becomes a compliant one. This thought process brings the courage to enter into the transactions that the business owners believe the government may raise questions about in the future. For example, a business dealer has purchased the vehicle for personal use in the name of the business and claims the Input Tax Credit while filing the GST returns, despite the fact that his consultant has denied the same. The thought process that backs the decision to claim the Input Tax Credit is *"Ek baar ITC lekar dekh lete hain, agar notice aya toh reverse kar denge, thoda bahut interest hi toh pay karna padega. Lekin agar notice nahi aya toh ITC ka benefit mil jayega."*

This thought process is deprived of the knowledge that claiming the ITC is prohibited by the law, which sends a message to the government that the dealer has the mindset to claim the ITC, which is not permissible under the law. The government or revenue authorities heavily depend on the "INTENTION" of the dealer while deciding the course of action and quantum of relief to be provided to the dealer in case of assessment proceedings. In case the dealer fails to establish that the non-compliance is unintentional, the government may grant relief. Still, suppose the dealer fails to make the government believe that the non-compliance was unintentional. In that case, the government will take all the extreme measures for the recovery proceedings and will initiate the penalty proceedings. The business dealer must keep in mind that the government is recording every action, and they are using the same to understand the intention of the dealer. So, every mistake counts, and paying the interest and penalty only makes the default good; it doesn't convert the non-compliant dealer into a compliant one in the eyes of the law.

So, Prtithvi, above are a few of the common myths that prevail in the mindset of business owners. Once the business owners get rid of these, they will find themselves more focused on being compliant dealers.

P: Indeed, you share a very insightful knowledge, Sir. Now that you have educated me about the impact of non-compliance and its gravity, along with the myths, I am curious to know what a businessman can do to avoid non-compliance. Is it very difficult to become a compliant dealer?

V: Absolutely not, Prithvi. One must be aware and committed to being a compliant dealer, and then the actions of the business owners must be within the boundaries of Compliance.

P: Sir, please explain this in detail so that I can amend my current prevailing business practices and avoid any non-compliance.

V: You are required to take very simple actions, and I will explain them in detail.

CHAPTER 5

HOW TO AVOID NON-COMPLIANCE

Vikas: Prithvi, it's not about doing great things or maintaining very strict business practices to make you compliant. Rather, you can be compliant by adopting a few good habits, and then those habits will dictate your actions. Let me tell you in detail:

1. Respect the timelines

This is the most important aspect of Compliance. If you start respecting the timelines, you will find that your business practices are aligned with the due dates decided by the government. Once the flow of business practices is aligned with the government due dates, you will find that you are able to comply with minimal effort. Also, if you respect the due dates, it automatically results in effective time management, completion of tasks within time limits, and professionalism and reliability. It also helps prioritize tasks and allocate tasks effectively, avoids procrastination, and ensures time-effective business practices. Your team will always be driven and inspired by your commitment to consistently filing your returns ahead of time. Your team will look upon you as a dedicated professional who stands by their promises and always delivers on their commitments.

So, if you choose to adopt, you will always respect the timelines. Your business practices will be so time-effective and efficient that you will easily avoid interest, penalties, and unwanted litigation.

2. <u>Get informed through Professionals only.</u>

Today, we have multiple platforms to gather knowledge. Although it is a good scenario that one can be educated by multiple means of schools, the catch is, how can you be sure that the information being communicated to you is accurate and trustworthy? If you rely on the wrong information and act upon it, you might end up losing, whether in terms of money or any other loss.

For example, suppose you want to register for GST in Noida, and you have searched for it on Google. In that case, you will get the list of documents required for GST Registration, but you might not know that the stamp duty rate is 2% for the rent agreement of the business premises.

You applied for the GST registration using the rent agreement notarized on the stamp paper of Rs. 100, and your registration was rejected due to the improper rent agreement. So, you have delayed your registration by a minimum.

By 15 days, the reason is that it relies on incomplete information. Therefore, business owners must get information from professionals only, which will allow for effective decision-making.

We are getting regular updates from various sources regarding do's and don'ts, changes in due dates, relaxations, or additions in data for return filing.

Still, one must discuss and confirm the authenticity of the information from the professionals before relying upon it.

Any information from unknown sources must be authenticated before being considered in decision-making to avoid monetary or non-monetary losses.

3. <u>Training of Employees</u>

Business owners must understand the fact that every industry has its working style, and employees must be trained accordingly if they want to achieve results. Training of employees is a must to foster a learning culture and create an effective workforce. Employees must be updated with the amendments and new statutory requirements so that they have time and knowledge to amend their business processes to comply with the statutory requirements effectively. Ultimately, it's the workforce that performs the operations at the ground level. If they are adequately trained with a clear vision of the business organization, they will walk hand in hand with the organization.

So, train the employees in such a manner that they have thoroughly adopted our policy of Compliance, and no lapses in Compliance must be there due to a lack of knowledge.

4. <u>Creating an Effective Business System</u>

When business owners are aware of the business's goals, they create a whole system that encourages everyone to achieve those goals. Similarly, business owners must create business systems that consider all the required aspects of Compliance. Systems must ensure that all the inputs required for Compliance are gathered on time and processed well before the due date.

The following is the illustrative framework of an effective business system:

1. **An annual compliance calendar** should be available with the business organization, and all the due timelines **must be incorporated into the business systems**. For example, sales invoice data must be compiled within 5 days of the completion of the month. And the sales team must submit their sales report to the accounts team by the 3rd of the succeeding month so that the accounts team has sufficient time to process the data effectively and efficiently.

2. **The flow of information** within the organization must be decided so precisely that all information **must reach the concerned person before the due date**. Suppose the procurement invoices are not provided to the accounts team on time. In that case, he will not be able to provide the correct input tax credit report to the chartered accountant or any professional filing the GST returns, which will result

in a wrong ITC claim amount. So, the system for the flow of information must be clearly defined, and no lapses should be allowed in this system.

3. One of the major gaps in the organization is that they don't **ask for acknowledgment** for the data shared with the professional. This is a major lapse since the professional must be receiving the data from a number of clients; they might miss the mail you sent. So, it is advised to ask for acknowledgment from the professional about whether they have received the data or not, and it will also serve as a reminder to the professional. In addition, I advise my clients to keep a copy of the acknowledgment for every return filed. This will also be a check to see if the return has been filed and if there is no mismatch in the Compliance.

4. Data must be handled by the concerned person only. With this, please take care of the fact that the data must be reached and handled only by the concerned personnel. This will decrease the time for information to travel, and data will be processed on time, which will result in the timely generation of reports. For example, if purchase invoices are

kept in the custody of the marketing team, they will be limited to record-keeping only. Only when the invoices are handed over to the accounts team, working on ITC, booking the invoice in the books of accounts, payment-related documents, etc., will be done. So, make sure that the data is only shared with the concerned personnel.

P: Vikas, I feel a strong urgency to adopt the key principles needed for building an effective business system. First, we often lack the precise thinking and planning required to design such systems. Second, we tend to fall short when it comes to executing those systems with the consistency and focus they truly demand.

V: Prithvi, to become successful in business, you don't need to do different things—you need to do things differently. It's the approach that makes all the difference. And believe me, you save so much by creating the systems to be compliant that you can't even calculate.

CHAPTER 6

COMPLIANCE: AN INVESTMENT, NOT A BURDEN

Vikas: I have discussed non-compliance and its impacts with you in detail, but have I ever mentioned how economical it is to be a compliant business owner?

Prithvi: No, but you just spoke my mind. You have enlightened me about non-compliance and its impact in detail, but have you ever mentioned the expense of being a compliant business owner?

Vikas: Prithvi, we will do an analysis right now. Then, you will tell me whether being compliant is expensive or economical. You will rate the risk weightage attached to my questions, and we will award the marks/points accordingly.

The following is the system for rewarding points for the

answers:

a) Cost/ Loss is easily bearable – 3 points

b) Cost/Loss is difficult to bear- 5 points

c) Cost/Loss is heavy and will impact the going concern - 7 points

d) Cost/Loss can't be ascertained – 10 points. So, here are the questions for you.

S. No.	Question (By ViKas)	Answer (By Prithvi)	Marks
1	Loss of Money due to non-compliance	Option- B	5
2	Loss of Productivity in the business	Option- B	5
3	Loss of Goodwill	Option- C	7
4	Loss of Mental Peace and health due to uncertainty of levy of demand	Option- D	10

| 5 | Loss of Trust of Customers, Suppliers, Banks, and related parties | Option- D | 10 |

Now, let's analyze the above response from the business owner's point of view. We can easily conclude that a business owner can somehow manage the loss of money by paying additional taxes, interest, and penalties, along with professional expenses for litigation, etc. Although this will squeeze the profit margins significantly, the loss is still bearable from the business point of view. Although it is not easy to ascertain the loss of productivity, it can also be borne by the business owner.

However, we found that it is difficult to handle the loss of goodwill and a bad name for the brand due to non-compliance. It is not easy to ascertain the impact of non-compliance on the business organization's goodwill in monetary terms.

Loss of trust among clients, suppliers, bankers, and other stakeholders is immeasurable. This means that loss of trust might result in an indefinite loss of business because the business is based on relations with other parties in the market. If you lose the trust factor, it becomes quite difficult to run a business organization. As we know, if you do good all the time, you might be ignored for recognition, but if you bring a bad name for any reason, you will be remembered for that for a very long time. That is the mindset of the society. In such a scenario, building trust again is an uphill task. So, loss of trust is a major setback, and one can't ascertain the cost of the same to the business.

And the most threatening loss for the business is the loss of mental peace, the loss of health, and the loss of trust from the related parties, which is caused by non-compliance. It is not easy to ascertain the loss of mental peace complications caused in the body due to the increased stress and anxiety. The loss is massive, and the worst thing is that, in most cases, we completely ignore this aspect of loss. In general discussion, loss means loss of money in the business, and we fail to understand the gravity of the silent loss of mental peace and its impact on the health of the business owner. In some cases, we came across that the business owner suffered from a disease or two due to increased stress and anxiety. Moreover, it indirectly impacts the lives of the family members of the business owners. So, this by-product of non-compliance might create havoc in the lives of the business person, and knowingly or unknowingly, we choose to ignore this.

V: So, Prithvi, I would now like to hear your verdict—would you say that non-compliance proves to be more costly or economical?"

Prithvi: Being Compliant is always economical, and that is certain. The fact is, we don't assess the impact of non-compliance so deeply, so we were not in a position to evaluate the cost of non-compliance. But now I think, instead of ascertaining the cost of non-compliance, it is much better to get the quotation from you for Compliance, which you will be taking care of from now on for my business.

Vikas: Prithvi, you are a close friend of Akash, who happens to be a very dear client of mine. More than a client, he is part of my extended family. So, whatever knowledge we have shared today is to make you aware of the importance of Compliance. Let me tell you about the ***X-factor of being a compliant business owner*** before sharing the quotation.

CHAPTER 7

X-FACTOR OF COMPLIANCE

Vikas: Prithvi, being compliant, offers a bouquet of benefits that every business owner must know about. Let me discuss a few of them that business owners commonly experience.

1. <u>Establishing Credibility through Compliance</u>

Compliant business owners carry a sense of authority in comparison to non-compliant business owners. There is one incident that I came across, and I realized what authority-building compliances do for the business. The GST Department detained a vehicle due to a clerical mistake in the invoice of the goods being carried in the vehicle. My client visited the GST office for the release of the vehicle and requested the officer to release the vehicle since the mistake was a clerical error and there was no intention of tax evasion. Then my client said, *"Sir, my company is 21 years old;*

you may check the compliance history of my company from day one. My company is unscathed in terms of Compliance. If you detain the goods just because of a clerical mistake, the legacy carried by my company will be dented. So, I request you to please release the vehicle and allow my company to be unscathed in terms of Compliance." The officer considered the statement very positively and agreed to release the vehicle. Making such a huge statement in the GST office is the impact of confidence that a business owner must have after being compliant. Such confidence and credibility are enjoyed only by compliant business owners.

2. <u>Impression in the eyes of the law</u>

The government, in the form of regulatory bodies, keeps a close eye on the business owners through the systems they develop to scrutinize the returns filed, and they also keep track of the activities performed at the GST Portal. They have a rating system in which the government rates the business owners as excellent, good, average, or below average on the basis of Compliance. They also identify business owners who are risky to society and the government. Revenue authorities have a relaxed approach for those business dealers who fall under the category of good or excellent compliant business dealers. So, being compliant creates a good impression in the eyes of the law, which helps business owners to avoid unwanted litigation.

3. <u>Helps in fundraising</u>

This benefit is huge, and it must have been experienced by the business owners that the lender, which may be a bank or any other financial institution, checks the Compliance before processing the application for raising funds. If the banks or lending institutions find that you are a compliant dealer, then it helps them make decisions in favor of the business owner. Being compliant also sends the message regarding the intention of the client, and once the intention is proven to be good, it's easy for the lenders to take the call in favor of the business owners.

4. <u>Unlocking New Opportunities Through a Culture of Compliance</u>

A business owner can go for expansion only when he is compliant. If the business owner is non-compliant, he will be stuck in a never-ending loop of operations, filing the returns, receiving the notices, submitting a reply, getting the order, and deciding on a further course of action. One must have a free mind in order to think clearly, plan, and execute the necessary course of action for expansion purposes. A distracted mind, which is always stuck in making past actions good in the present, can't afford the luxury of having a robust mindset, which is required for business expansion. Therefore, if you want to grow your business in the future, then your present business system must be so effective in terms of Compliance that it should take care of Compliance on its own, and you have to give minimal time and effort for the same.

5.   <u>Partner in the Growth of the Country</u>

This fact is highly underrated; if the business owners play their part with integrity and always act as law-abiding business dealers, then they are actually partners in the growth of the country. Serving the country doesn't require you to be in uniform only and serve at the border; any person who is fulfilling their duties with complete dedication and integrity is actually serving the country.

Every business owner is a partner in the growth of the country, and if you are a compliant dealer, you can actually have that feeling without any ifs or buts.

The beauty lies in the fact that you are not doing anything special to serve the motherland; you are just doing your business compliances as they are mandatorily required to be done, and you are a partner in the growth of our country.

Vikas: Now, it's completely your choice to be a business owner only or to be a business owner who is also a partner in the growth of the country.

Prithvi: Vikas, you have imparted knowledge and awareness in such an amazing manner that taking a call is very easy. I have decided that I will not only be a business owner but also a partner in the growth of our country. Also, I have decided to remain connected with you, and you will be taking care of my business compliance.

Prithvi then called his friend Akash and thanked him for getting Prithvi connected with Vikas ji. Prithvi also promised himself that he would apply the knowledge he got and create an effective business system with an inbuilt, well-knit compliance calendar.

Prithvi has already started the journey toward becoming a compliant business owner. What about you???

*Here's a **GST Compliance Chart** covering the key compliance requirements under the Goods and Services Tax (GST) regime:

Compliance	Form	Frequency	Due Date	Applicable To
GSTR-1 (Outward Supplies)	GSTR-1	Monthly / Quarterly	11th of next month / 13th of next month (for QRMP)	Regular taxpayers
GSTR-3B (Summary Return)	GSTR-3B	Monthly / Quarterly	20th of next month / Staggered for QRMP	Regular taxpayers

GSTR-4 (Composition Scheme)	GSTR-4	Annually	30th April (next FY)	Composition taxpayers
GSTR-5 (Non-Resident Taxpayer)	GSTR-5	Monthly	20th of next month	Non-resident taxable persons
GSTR-6 (Input Service Distributor)	GSTR-6	Monthly	13th of next month	ISDs
GSTR-7 (TDS Return)	GSTR-7	Monthly	10th of next month	TDS deductors under GST
GSTR-8 (TCS Return)	GSTR-8	Monthly	10th of next month	E-commerce operators
Annual Return	GSTR-9	Annually	31st December (next FY)	Registered taxpayers (turnover > ₹2 Cr)

Reconciliation Statement	GSTR-9C	Annually	31st December (next FY)	Registered taxpayers (audit applicable)
Letter of Undertaking (LUT)	LUT	Annually	Before the start of FY	Exporters without payment of tax
Payment of Tax	PMT-06	Monthly / Quarterly	20th / Due as per QRMP	All GST taxpayers

CALL TO ACTION

To Make Your Business Compliant, Scan And Connect With Me